T0365339

Tinker's Chicks

Book One

Written by

Kristie Burrill

I dedicate my book to my father, Leon Merritt Burrill, who always thought I should pursue a writing career. And to Miss Love, my high school writing teacher. She gave me an "F" on my first essay, but an "A" for the term, because she grades on improvement.

Copyright © 2016 by Kristie Burrill. 731823

ISBN: Softcover   978-1-5144-4989-9
       EBook   978-1-5144-4988-2

Print information available on the last page

Rev. date: 02/05/2016

To order additional copies of this book, contact:
Xlibris
1-888-795-4274
www.Xlibris.com
Orders@Xlibris.com

Contents

Chapter 1

How We Met

cheep, cheap, cheap, cheep? I'm confused!

I'd heard that it's cheap, easy, and fun to raise egg-laying chickens in the city.

The garden shed in my fenced backyard was the perfect place.

A limit of three chicks is allowed in the city, but no roosters— too noisy too early in the morning.

It was less than $20.00 to purchase the newly hatched "fluff balls," the feed, and feeders.

I kept the chicks indoors in a cage with a heat lamp to keep them warm. They were content to eat, sleep, chirp, play, eat, sleep, chirp, and play all day and all night. I was annoyed, but Tinker was intrigued.

She'd watch them for long periods of time, never slipping her paws into the cage. Often, she'd drape herself over the round top of the cage, watching them in silence.

I introduced the chicks to some children so they could each pick one to name.

The yellow chick was named Daisy; the multicolored one, Maizey; and the black one, Omelette.

"Why Omelette?" I asked.

"Because isn't that what you're going to make with her eggs?"

Can't argue with that!

As the chicks grew and tried to establish a pecking order, the endless noise became louder and louder. Tinker's catnaps were constantly interrupted when she scurried to check on the chicks— her chicks.

Once the chicks' tail feathers grew in and poked through the cage, Tinker's curiosity got the best of her.

"Aren't these feathers like a kitty toy?"

One sharp peck on the nose and her question was answered.

After six weeks, I moved the chicks to the backyard. I was thrilled, but Tinker was worried. She followed them everywhere, kept them in sight, and then rounded them up like a border collie. I find her behavior unusual for a cat, but really no different than the

lion that lay with the lamb.

The chicks were getting bigger and more independent, much to Tinker's dismay, as they are now faster and are able to fly.

Maizey

Daisy

Omelette

They have different personalities, yet all run to greet me at the gate. Maizey and Daisy like me to stroke their feathers.

"The time is almost near for the first egg to appear. Will it be white,

brown, oblong, round, or square? I guess we'll have to wait, but I know what I will make—a very tasty omelette to grace my breakfast plate."

What will you make?

Chapter 2

The First Egg

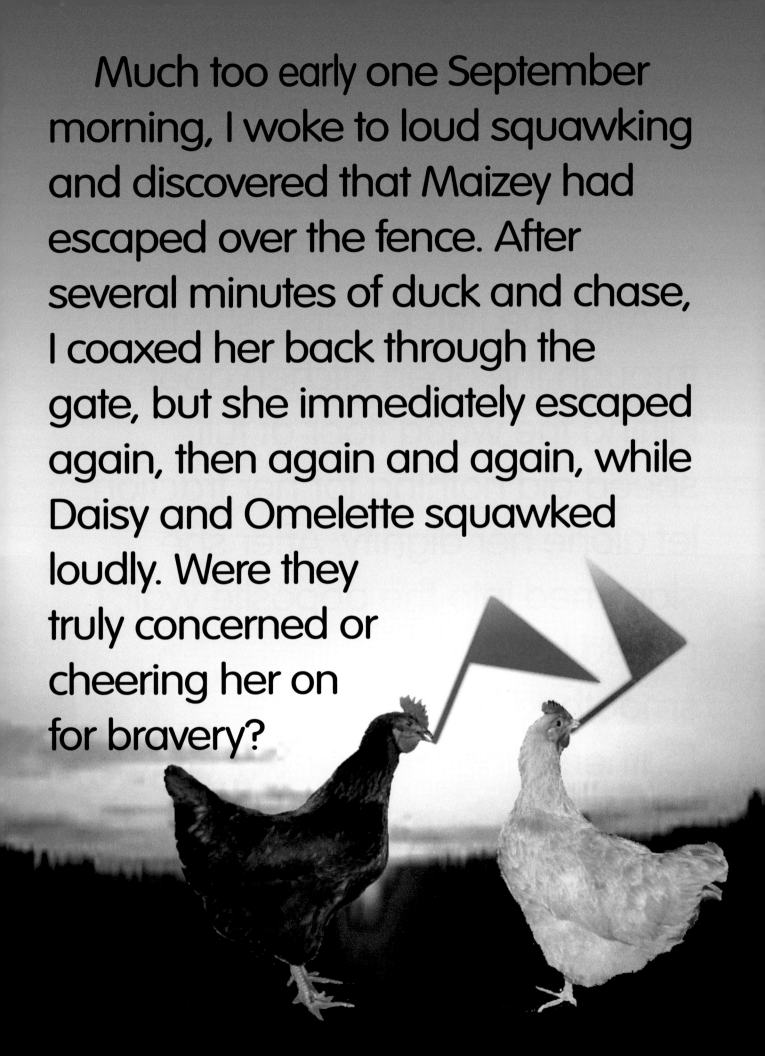

Much too early one September morning, I woke to loud squawking and discovered that Maizey had escaped over the fence. After several minutes of duck and chase, I coaxed her back through the gate, but she immediately escaped again, then again and again, while Daisy and Omelette squawked loudly. Were they truly concerned or cheering her on for bravery?

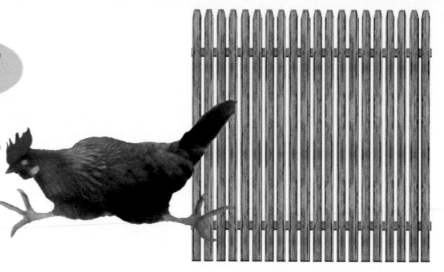

After the fifth escape, she ran through the open kitchen door. Hitting the wood floor at full speed did nothing for her traction, let alone her dignity. After she slammed into the opposite wall, I picked her up, smoothed her feathers, and once again put her through the gate.

After the sixth escape and return, my patience was wearing thin, so I followed her. She ran through the backyard, climbed the tree, and hopped to the top of the fence, then down to the ground. For me, the chase was over. There must be a valid reason for her behavior. Twenty minutes later, I found her under a bush. She seemed calm and content, so I left her there.

The next time I checked, she was not alone. An elongated white egg lay under her. I picked it up, thanked her, and opened the gate.

She scurried through without hesitation and was joyfully greeted by Omelette and Daisy.

I placed her egg on the floor of the shed and all the girls

gathered around to inspect it.
I know we'll go through this again before the other two lay their first egg. I only hope I get a clue as to where, before they spoil.

The next morning,  Maizey escaped over the fence, again. After I escorted her through the gate, she disappeared for hours. I checked her first nesting spot, but she wasn't there, so I decided to wait for a while. Eventually, my concern prompted a thorough yard search on both sides of the fence. Daisy and Omelette followed me with squawking concern, yet gave no clue as to Maizey's whereabouts.

After some subtle clucking

on my part, thankful the neighbors weren't home to hear, a similar sound came from under the shed. I got down on my hand and knees and saw Maizey nesting. With rake in hand, I coaxed her out. She scurried off, her work was done. A second sweep of the

rake produced a perfect white egg, but I blocked off the space, anyway.

This is not what I had in mind when I brought the three tiny "fluff balls" home. I envisioned a fun hobby and lots of organic eggs to enhance my health and give to family and friends.

No "cliché" nests for us. We're going to lay our eggs where we want, like Maizey.

The nests I created in the shed sit empty. I feel unappreciated!

I arrived home the next evening with no egg-spectations and received the usual greeting from the girls. A few feet away, with no trace of a shell, lay a round yellow yolk in the grass. It seemed so odd, that all I could imagine was a photo of it, tastefully framed and overly priced in an artsy gallery.

$3,500.00

We deliver !

My dream of fame and fortune in the gallery business lost priority when I spotted a large brown egg a few feet away.

It might take some time to coax the girls to accept their nests, so in the meantime, I'll have a daily egg hunt.

Chapter 3

The Egg Hunt

After the excitement of finding the first three eggs, I was ready to hunt for more, but the girls stopped laying eggs for several weeks. I was confused and frustrated.

I used those eggs for my homemade almond chocolate ice cream. Maybe they thought that was enough of a contribution.

I walk by the eggs in the grocery store but don't buy them. I'd feel like a traitor, an "Eggs Benedict Arnold." I'm really craving a three-minute soft one with salt and pepper.
When I confront the girls in the yard, they follow me, pecking at my shoes and clucking demands as if I am the one not delivering. Right now, I don't know eggs-actually what to do.

I was on the verge of "egg withdrawal" when I saw Maizey emerge from the recently blocked-off shed, but from the other side.

Down on my knees again, with rake in hand, I retrieved a green tennis ball. The next two sweeps produced three white and four brown eggs. I was thrilled but blocked off that side of the shed too.

The next day, I was home sick, so didn't care where the girls laid their eggs. I lay in bed listening to their loud squawking, a sign they were about to shoot 'em out. I really hope they aim for the egg carton in the refrigerator.

Finally, feeling better, I got out of bed and found a large brown egg just inside the  gate and Maizey and Omelette with anticipation of praise. Maizey lays white eggs and Daisy is always the first to greet me, so I knew it was Omelette's egg. Daisy, however, was nowhere in sight. Then Tinker meowed from the roof of the shed.

Without hesitation, she hopped from the roof over the fence and into the neighbor's yard. When I entered the yard, Tinker looked up at me then back down at the foliage. I heard a cluck and underneath the foliage was Daisy with a large brown egg.

The neighbors appeared and said they'd found her in their yard earlier and put her back over the fence, because their dachshund was barking at her. I knew he wasn't a threat, but I'm sure he felt like a big dog for a minute.

WOOF ?

When I arrived home that night, both Daisy and Maizey were in the neighbor's yard, no dog, but a large Maine coon cat  named Tanker was quietly watching them.

It's time to clip their wing feathers so they can't fly over the fence. I really want the girls to stay home.

I envisioned myself like Martha Stewart, without the money and jail time, walking out the kitchen door with a basket on my arm to collect

eggs. Calculating the minimal cost to buy and raise the chicks, no problem. Lots of fun, lots of eggs . . . cheap, cheep.

Calculating the time spent hunting eggs, blocking off unsatisfactory nesting areas, retrieving eggs from the neighbor's yard, the cost of each egg is equal to one by Faberge.

But the experience, joy, and entertainment while raising our chickens—priceless!

Printed in the United States
By Bookmasters